RETURN FROM EXTINCTION

THE AMERICAN BISON

LEONARD CLASKY

Gareth Stevens Publishing

Please visit our website, www.garethstevens.com. For a free color catalog of all our high-quality books, call toll free 1-800-542-2595 or fax 1-877-542-2596.

Portions of this work were originally authored by Theresa Morlock and published as *The Return of the American Bison.* All new material this edition authored by Leonard Clasky.

Library of Congress Cataloging-in-Publication Data

Names: Clasky, Leonard, author.
Title: The American bison / Leonard Clasky.
Description: New York : Gareth Stevens Publishing, [2023] | Series: Return from extinction | Includes index. | Audience: Grades 4-6
Identifiers: LCCN 2021060494 (print) | LCCN 2021060495 (ebook) | ISBN 9781538280218 (library binding) | ISBN 9781538280195 (paperback) | ISBN 9781538280201 (set) | ISBN 9781538280225 (ebook)
Subjects: LCSH: American bison–United States–Juvenile literature. | American bison–Conservation–Juvenile literature.
Classification: LCC QL737.U53 C595 2023 (print) | LCC QL737.U53 (ebook) | DDC 333.95/96430973–dc23/eng/20211215
LC record available at https://lccn.loc.gov/2021060494
LC ebook record available at https://lccn.loc.gov/2021060495

Published in 2023 by
Gareth Stevens Publishing
29 E. 21st Street
New York, NY 10010

Designer: Olivia Lo Sardo
Editor: Caitie McAneney

Photo credits: Cover, IngerErikson/Shutterstock; p4-5, Mikadun/Shutterstock; p6, VladSokolovsky/Shutterstock; p7, ScottCanning/Shutterstock.com; p9 https://en.wikipedia.org/wiki/File:Bison_skull_pile_edit.jpg; p10, riekephotos/Shutterstock; p11, ValerieWei-Haas/Shutterstock; p12-13, p14-15 EveretteCollection/Shutterstock; p16 Maps/Shutterstock; p17, GabiLuka/Shutterstock; p18 GreyMountainPhoto/Shutterstock; p19 Manuel AS/Shutterstock; p20 SzezpanKlajbuk/Shutterstock; p21, KrisDurlen/Shutterstock; p22-23, MeganBrady/Shutterstock; p25 Robert Brown Stock/Shutterstock; p27 RichardGSmith/Shutterstock

Printed in the United States of America

CPSIA compliance information: Batch #CSGS23: For further information contact Gareth Stevens, New York, New York at 1-800-542-2595.

CONTENTS

Words in the glossary appear in **bold** type the first time they are used in the text.

A MIGHTY MAMMAL

The American bison is the national **mammal** of the United States. And yet, it was hunted nearly to **extinction** by white settlers in the 1800s. The actions of these settlers nearly erased the bison from the American landscape.

From prehistoric times, American bison roamed the U.S. Great Plains, numbering in the millions. Plains Indians treated them with respect and honor. But that changed in the 1800s when white settlers stole Native Peoples' land, targeted bison, and limited bison **habitats** by building railroads. By the 1900s, bison were on the brink of extinction. Today, **conservation** efforts have brought populations up to around 30,000.

Many bison were hunted purely for sport. Some settlers felt they were in the way of the American vison of progress.

GREAT PLAINS PEOPLES

HUMANS HAVE LIVED ON THE GREAT PLAINS FOR AT LEAST 10,000 YEARS, OR EVEN AS MANY AS 38,000 YEARS, SIDE-BY-SIDE WITH BISON. NATIVE PEOPLES OF THE U.S. GREAT PLAINS INCLUDE THE LAKOTA, DAKOTA, AND CHEYENNE. THEY ONLY KILLED BISON WHEN THEY NEEDED TO, AND THEY USED THE ANIMALS FOR FOOD, CLOTHING, SHELTER, AND TOOLS. THEY BELIEVED THE BISON GAVE THEM LIFE.

MEET THE BISON

Of all the land mammals in North America, the American bison tops the charts for size. They can weigh up to 2,200 pounds (998 kg) and stand 6 feet (1.8 m) tall. They spend most of their time roaming the Great Plains and grazing—or eating—grasses, herbs, shrubs, and twigs.

Bison have special **adaptations**. A bison's thick coat of fur makes it well adapted to the snowy winters of the Great Plains. They also have very good senses of smell and hearing. Bison can run at speeds up to about 40 miles (64.4 km) per hour. Additionally, they have sharp horns that can grow up to 2 feet (0.6 m) long.

BISON ADAPTATIONS

Bison are often called "buffalo." However, they are a different animal from the true buffalo living in Asia and Africa.

BISON HERDS

ONE BISON ADAPTATION IS LIVING TOGETHER IN HERDS, WHICH HELPS THEM **MIGRATE** FOR FOOD. FEMALES ARE CALLED COWS, AND MALES ARE CALLED BULLS. A FEMALE BISON GIVES BIRTH ONCE A YEAR DURING THE SPRING. BISON ONLY HAVE ONE BABY AT A TIME, WHICH IS CALLED A CALF OR "RED-DOG" (FOR ITS COLOR). SOME HERDS INCLUDE THOUSANDS OF BISON!

A PART OF THE PLAINS

For much of history, bison were an important part of the Plains. In the days of the great bison herds, when Plains Indians killed a bison, they didn't waste any part of the bison's body. Plains Indians had over 150 uses for bison parts. They used bison skins and furs to make their shelter, and used bones for tools. Bison populations were stable.

When European settlers arrived, they built farms and railroads, dividing up the lands that the bison had once roamed freely. The settlers also introduced **domesticated** cattle, which gave bison new diseases. Bison were treated as pests and not as sacred, or holy, creatures.

A SACRED ANIMAL

MANY PLAINS INDIANS INCLUDING THE CHEROKEE, LAKOTA, AND DAKOTA FELT THAT THE BISON WAS A POWERFUL, HOLY BEING. THEY VALUED THE BISON NOT ONLY BECAUSE IT PROVIDED THEM WITH THE TOOLS TO SURVIVE BUT ALSO BECAUSE IT WAS A GREAT CREATURE. MANY DANCES, PRAYERS, AND STORIES CELEBRATE THE BISON. TODAY, BISON ARE STILL IMPORTANT PARTS OF PLAINS INDIAN **CULTURE.**

When settlers first arrived, there were about 40 million bison. By the late 1800s, there were only about 300 to 450. This photograph shows a pile of bison skulls in 1892.

HUNTED FOR HIDES

One reason white settlers killed bison was for the fur trade. Bison were hunted for their hides, or skin and fur. During the 18th and 19th centuries, settlers killed thousands of bison for the fur trade. Native Americans also hunted bison so they could trade hides for European goods and tools. Those hides were sold to markets.

Bison hides were very popular because they could be made into warm robes and coats. Many U.S. soldiers wore bison coats during the winter. They were also popular in European fashions of the time. Other animals killed for the fur trade were bears, rabbits, foxes, elk, and wolves.

These furs are shown at the Hudson's Bay Company in Langley, Canada.

THE HUDSON'S BAY COMPANY

THE HUDSON'S BAY COMPANY IS A CANADIAN COMPANY THAT PLAYED A LARGE PART IN THE FUR TRADE. IN 1844, THE HUDSON'S BAY COMPANY REPORTED THAT 75,000 BISON ROBES WERE TRADED TO POSTS IN CANADA. AS TIME WENT ON, PEOPLE DISCOVERED BETTER METHODS OF CLEANING HIDES, WHICH MADE PEOPLE WANT THEM MORE.

MOVING WEST

Europeans first settled the eastern part of North America. But the early 1800s saw them move west in rising numbers. Driven by the promise of land and gold, settlers stole land from Native Peoples. When conflicts arose, settlers felt that Native Americans stood in the way of their progress.

White settlers knew that Plains Indians relied on bison to survive. So settlers hunted bison in an effort to starve out Plains Indians and drive them from their homelands. White settlers killed immense numbers of bison to force out the Plains Indians. They used the bison to feed railroad workers and army soldiers—and left Plains Indians to starve.

The U.S. government led forces against Native Peoples across the continent, killing many people and forcing others to live on **reservations**.

MANIFEST DESTINY

BY 1845, WESTWARD EXPANSION WASN'T JUST SEEN AS AMERICANS' RIGHT, IT WAS THEIR DESTINY. MANIFEST DESTINY WAS THE IDEA THAT THE UNITED STATES SETTLERS SHOULD SPREAD THEIR VALUES AND SYSTEMS TO ALL OF NORTH AMERICA. THEY SAW THIS AS THEIR GOD-GIVEN RIGHT AND WOULDN'T LET ANYTHING OR ANYONE STAND IN THEIR WAY.

HUNT BY RAIL

In 1863, the United States started building the first railroad to stretch across North America: the transcontinental railroad. When it was completed in 1869, people could travel coast to coast by rail for the first time. It also played a major part in the mass killing of bison.

Some people traveled west just to take part in bison hunts. Men shot bison from train windows as they passed herds. The railroads sold trips to "hunt by rail." New developments in firearms made it possible to kill more bison than ever before. Railroads also made it easier to trade bison hides and meat.

Though fast and strong, the bison were no match for the hunters' guns. The bison skull became a symbol, or sign, of the Wild West.

FAMOUS BISON HUNTERS

SOME PEOPLE BECAME FAMOUS FOR HUNTING BISON. HUNTER ORLANDO BROWN KILLED NEARLY 6,000 BISON HIMSELF. WILLIAM "BUFFALO BILL" CODY BECAME FAMOUS FOR BISON HUNTING DURING THE LATE 1860s. IN 1867, CODY HUNTED THOUSANDS OF BISON TO FEED THE WORKERS BUILDING THE KANSAS PACIFIC RAILROAD. LATER, HE BECAME A NATIONAL FOLK HERO AFTER STARTING BUFFALO BILL'S WILD WEST SHOW.

DIVIDING THE HERD

As settlers populated and built up the West, bison habitats quickly shrank. The transcontinental railroad also divided the Great Plains bison into two herds: a northern herd and a southern herd. The northern herd had more room to roam, but the southern herd had more bison in it. More than 3 million bison made up this southern herd in 1871. But between 1871 and 1875, the southern herd was completely wiped out.

After the extinction of the southern herd, the population of the northern herd continued to drop. By 1883, the northern herd was also wiped out. Only fewer than 1,000 bison were left, in small bands.

RANGE OF THE AMERICAN BISON BEFORE EUROPEAN SETTLEMENT

RANGE OF THE AMERICAN BISON TODAY

WEAK LAWS

LAWS PROTECTING BISON WERE OFTEN TOO WEAK OR TOO LATE. IN 1864, THE IDAHO STATE GOVERNMENT PASSED A BISON PROTECTION LAW, BUT IDAHO'S BISON HAD ALREADY BEEN WIPED OUT. IN 1874, A FEDERAL BILL WAS INTRODUCED TO MAKE IT ILLEGAL FOR ANY NON-NATIVE AMERICAN TO KILL OR HARM A FEMALE BISON OR KILL A MALE NEEDLESSLY. HOWEVER, THIS BILL WAS NEVER SIGNED INTO LAW.

Today, wild bison roam only around 1 percent of their historical range, or the areas they occupied before they were nearly hunted to extinction.

BISON AND BIODIVERSITY

Every living thing in an **ecosystem** plays an important role, or part. When animals die out, an ecosystem suffers. American bison were important to the Great Plains ecosystem. By stomping the soil with their hooves and by wallowing, or rolling around in the dirt, bison opened up space for seeds to settle and grow. They kept grasslands healthy by grazing as they moved. They left behind waste, which made soil richer.

Without bison, the ecosystem started to change. Cattle took their place and farms covered the once-wild grasslands, creating an unnatural landscape. And without bison wallowing, there was less biodiversity.

BIODIVERSITY

BIODIVERSITY IS THE VARIETY OF LIFE IN A PLACE. THE MORE BIODIVERSITY, THE HEALTHIER THE ECOSYSTEM. PLANTS AND ANIMALS PROVIDE FOOD, WATER, AND SHELTER TO ONE ANOTHER AND TO US. GREATER BIODIVERSITY, SUCH AS IN THE GREAT PLAINS, CAN ALSO MAKE THE AREA BETTER ABLE TO HANDLE **CLIMATE CHANGE**.

This bison is wallowing to cool off. Some people hope that bringing bison back to the Great Plains can help the natural ecosystem return to a healthier state.

CONSERVATION EFFORTS

There were few bison left when people started working to save them. Congress passed the first federal law concerned with protecting the American bison in 1894. This law punished anyone who killed bison with a $1,000 fine or prison time.

In 1905, President Theodore Roosevelt, William Hornaday, and other conservationists created the American Bison Society. The society's goal was to rescue bison populations by relocating herds to wildlife **refuges** where they would be protected from hunters. In 1907, the society shipped 15 bison from the Bronx Zoo to what is today the Wichita Mountains Wildlife Refuge in Oklahoma. These early conservation efforts set the stage for the bison's comeback.

THEODORE ROOSEVELT

THEODORE ROOSEVELT WAS PRESIDENT OF THE UNITED STATES FROM 1901 TO 1909. HE WAS VERY IMPORTANT TO THE CONSERVATION MOVEMENT. DURING HIS PRESIDENCY, HE WORKED TO PASS MANY LAWS TO PROTECT THE ENVIRONMENT AND SUFFERING SPECIES, INCLUDING BISON. HE SET ASIDE LANDS FOR NEW NATIONAL PARKS AND FORESTS IN THE WEST.

By 1935, the American Bison Society voted it was no longer needed.

THE BISON OF YELLOWSTONE

In 1872, the first national park was established in the United States. Yellowstone National Park covers land in Wyoming, Idaho, and Montana. This set off a movement across the world as other countries started making national parks too. Parks became places where animals could live in their natural environment, or surroundings.

Bison had lived in the Yellowstone area since prehistoric times. During the early 1900s, efforts to protect the bison in Yellowstone played a large role in their recovery throughout the United States. In 1902, there were only 24 bison left in Yellowstone. In 2021, there were between 2,300 to 5,500 bison in Yellowstone.

THE YELLOWSTONE HERD

THE YELLOWSTONE BISON ARE THE LARGEST BISON POPULATION ON PUBLIC LAND. THE NATIONAL PARKS SERVICE (NPS) ALLOWS THEM TO ROAM FREE AND WILD WITHIN THE PARK. THEY CAN ACT AS THEY NORMALLY WOULD HAVE BEFORE WHITE SETTLERS ARRIVED. HOWEVER, THE NPS SOMETIMES HAS TO CONTROL THE BISON POPULATION SO THEY DON'T COME IN CONTACT WITH CATTLE AT NEARBY RANCHES AND SPREAD DISEASE.

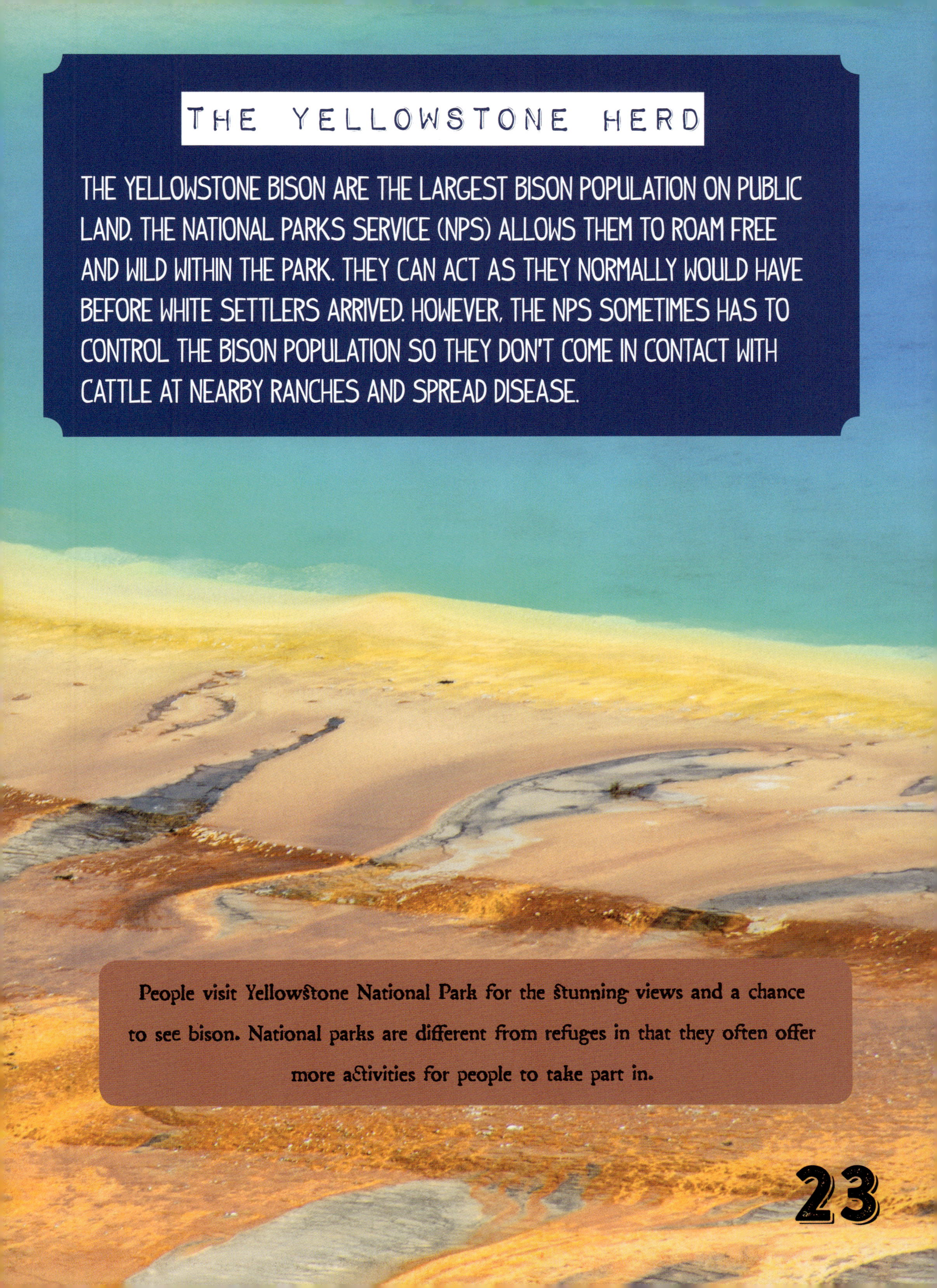

People visit Yellowstone National Park for the stunning views and a chance to see bison. National parks are different from refuges in that they often offer more activities for people to take part in.

PROTECTED POPULATIONS

The early 1900s saw more parks and refuges created across the United States. Within them, bison populations began to slowly recover. By 1910, the number of bison in North America had grown to about 2,100. By 1919, the population was about 12,500.

Native Americans played a huge role in bison recovery. In 1991, the InterTribal Buffalo Council, or ITBC, was formed. This council is made up of members of 69 tribes. Members work together to educate the public about bison and help create healthy bison herds. ITBC has restored more than 20,000 bison to tribal lands.

NATIONAL BISON RANGE

IN 1908, THE U.S. GOVERNMENT ESTABLISHED THE NATIONAL BISON RANGE IN MONTANA. BISON HAVE ABOUT 18,500 ACRES (7,486.7 HA) TO ROAM. ABOUT 350 TO 500 BISON LIVE ALONGSIDE BLACK BEARS, PRONGHORN ANTELOPES, ELK, AND BIGHORN SHEEP. PEOPLE CAN VISIT THE NATIONAL BISON RANGE, BUT THEY CAN'T HARM THE ANIMALS THERE.

At the National Bison Range in western Montana, bison can roam freely in their natural habitat.

A WAKE-UP CALL

The near-extinction of the American bison was a wake-up call to the United States. Before that, Americans didn't care much about harming wildlife and ecosystems as they settled land. Creating parks and refuges for bison was a necessary rescue mission. Laws were passed over time that limited bison hunting.

The near loss of bison taught many people that wildlife could not be treated so carelessly. The bison recovery programs and protection policies set an example for how other at-risk species should be treated in the United States. It marked a shift from caring little for the well-being of wildlife to working toward wildlife recovery.

THE ENDANGERED SPECIES ACT

IN 1973, PRESIDENT RICHARD NIXON SIGNED THE ENDANGERED SPECIES ACT TO PROTECT AT-RISK SPECIES FROM EXTINCTION. BISON WERE PROTECTED UNDER THIS ACT. BECAUSE OF THIS ACT, THE U.S. FISH AND WILDLIFE SERVICE KEEPS A LIST OF ENDANGERED (AT-RISK) SPECIES WORLDWIDE AND WORKS TO PROTECT THEM. IT ALSO MAKES SURE CERTAIN HABITATS AREN'T RUINED.

It's illegal to shoot and kill bison without a permit. However, Native People can hunt bison on their own lands.

WORK TO DO

Although bison populations have recovered, there's still more work to do. Their habitats are at risk from climate change and building projects. National parks must be protected and made larger to make sure that bison have the space and **resources** they need to survive.

The return of the American bison is a success story for conservation—even if it's not over yet. It shows that by working together and being aware of our effect on the environment, people can save species of animals from dying out. The American bison had a close call with extinction, but they will hopefully be around for many years to come.

A NATIONAL SYMBOL

PEOPLE HAVE OFTEN THOUGHT OF BISON AS A SYMBOL OF THE SPIRIT OF THE WEST. ON MAY 9, 2016, PRESIDENT BARACK OBAMA SIGNED THE NATIONAL BISON LEGACY ACT, MAKING THE AMERICAN BISON THE OFFICIAL NATIONAL MAMMAL OF THE UNITED STATES. THIS MADE PEOPLE MORE AWARE OF BISON AND THEIR HISTORIC COMEBACK.

Today American bison are called a keystone species. This means their population affects the health of other species in their ecosystem.

GLOSSARY

adaptation: A change in a type of animal that makes it better able to live in its surroundings.

climate change: Long-term change in Earth's climate, caused mainly by human activities such as burning oil and natural gas.

conservation: Efforts to care for the natural world.

culture: The beliefs and ways of life of a certain group of people.

domesticated: Bred and raised for use by people.

ecosystem: A natural community of living and nonliving things.

extinction: The death of all members of a species.

habitat: The natural place where an animal or plant lives.

mammal: A warm-blooded animal that has a backbone and hair, breathes air, and feeds milk to its young.

migrate: To move from one area to another for feeding or having babies.

refuge: A place set aside for wild animals to live safely.

reservation: Land set aside by the U.S. government for Native Americans.

resource: A usable supply of something.

FOR MORE INFORMATION

Books

Cooke, Tim. *A Scary Prediction: Bison Comeback.* Minneapolis, MN: Bearport Publishing, 2022.

Grunbaum, Mara. *Bison.* New York, NY: Children's Press, 2019.

O'Mara, John. *The Cheyenne (Native American Peoples).* New York, NY: Enslow Publishing, 2022.

Websites

American Bison
www.ducksters.com/animals/american_bison.php
Explore more fun facts about the American bison!

Native People of the American Great Plains
kids.nationalgeographic.com/history/article/native-people-of-the-american-great-plains
Learn more about the Plains Indians who lived side by side with the American bison for thousands of years.

Wildlife
www.nps.gov/yell/learn/kidsyouth/wildlife.htm
Discover the wildlife of Yellowstone National Park with the National Parks Service.

Publisher's note to educators and parents: Our editors have carefully reviewed these websites to ensure that they are suitable for students. Many websites change frequently, however, and we cannot guarantee that a site's future contents will continue to meet our high standards of quality and educational value. Be advised that students should be closely supervised whenever they access the Internet.

INDEX